KU-609-564

Take up Cricket

Principal contributor:
Ralph Middlebrook
Staff Coach, The National Cricket Association,
and Cricket Development Officer for the City of Leeds

SPRINGFIELD BOOKS LIMITED

ISBN 0 947655 58 1

First published 1989 by
Springfield Books Limited
Springfield House, Norman Road, Denby Dale, Huddersfield
HD8 8TH

Edited, designed and produced by
White Line Press
60 Bradford Road, Stanningley, Leeds LS28 6EF

Editors: Noel Whittall and Philip Gardner
Design: Krystyna Hewitt
Diagrams: Steve Beaumont and IT Design Associates

Printed and bound in Great Britain

Photographic credits
Cover photograph: Split Second
All other photographs by Noel Whittall

Acknowledgements
Our thanks to the cricketers who appear in the photographs:
Debra Maybury, Paul Grayson, Andrew Bairstow, and the
pupils of Fulneck School.

Contents

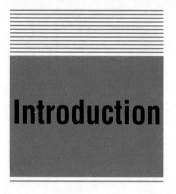

Introduction

Welcome to cricket! You have taken the first steps into one of the most fascinating sports in the world. This book will help you to get started the right way, and to make runs and take wickets from the beginning.

Getting started in cricket has never been easier. Although not all schools play it, the number of indoor centres is increasing rapidly, and in a number of countries a form of the game can be played throughout the year. There are lots of coaching schemes operated by clubs, local authorities and county associations, and teams at all levels are always on the lookout for new talent. Cricket isn't for men only; girls and women now make up a significant number of players, and mixed teams are a feature of many of the indoor leagues.

Throughout this book, we are mainly concerned with the standard game of cricket, as it has developed during the last two hundred years, and the junior version of that game. However, there are now many variations, chiefly those played indoors, and these are excellent ways of entry into the sport.

All games tend to change over a period of time, and cricket is no exception. For example, traditionalists may be surprised to find the expressions *batter* and *fielder* used in preference to *batsman* and *fieldsman*. The older styles are now often seen as inappropriate because so many girls and women now play cricket.

1

What *is* cricket?

Do you think of cricket as a bat and ball game? It's a lot more than that! Cricket is a game which calls for a wide variety of basic skills, which most of us can perform in some way without any training — most people can catch, throw, hit, shout and run. Cricket is only an organised extension of these skills. It is also a team game, where the fun of success is shared, and the satisfaction gained from good teamwork can make it far more rewarding than individual games. Quite apart from the enjoyment to be gained from playing in a full game, practising with a small group of friends can be great fun.

Cricket is played between two teams of eleven people. One team *bowls* and *fields* while two members of the other team *bat*; the player who is facing the bowling at any time is referred to as the *striker*. The object is for the batting team to gain as many *runs* as possible, while the bowling team tries to get the batters *out*. Later, the teams change places. This will all be explained shortly ...

The playing area

The cricket field comprises the *pitch* and the *outfield*. The *wickets* are set at each end of the pitch, which is normally close to the centre of the field. The overall size of the field is defined by a *boundary*. There is no set size for the field itself, but the boundary is usually a minimum of 75 yards (68 metres) from the *pitch*. It can be in the form of a line, a rope, a fence, or any other suitable feature.

The pitch is 22 yards (20.12 metres) long, and is marked at each end by two lines. These are the *bowling creases* and the *popping* or *batting creases*. Two further lines are marked at right angles to the bowling and popping creases: these are the *return creases*, the side limits for the bowler's feet.

Figure 1 The pitch (not to scale) — measurements are taken from the back edge of the crease

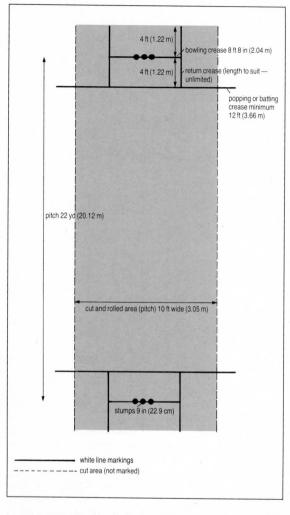

4 ft (1.22 m)

bowling crease 8 ft 8 in (2.04 m)

4 ft (1.22 m)

return crease (length to suit — unlimited)

popping or batting crease minimum 12 ft (3.66 m)

pitch 22 yd (20.12 m)

cut and rolled area (pitch) 10 ft wide (3.05 m)

stumps 9 in (22.9 cm)

————— white line markings

‒ ‒ ‒ ‒ ‒ ‒ ‒ ‒ ‒ ‒ cut area (not marked)

Figure 1 shows how the pitch should be marked out.

A *wicket* is placed at the centre of each bowling crease. Each wicket consists of three vertical *stumps*, upon which two *bails* are placed (Figure 2).

You will find that players and commentators use the word wicket very loosely: to be quite accurate, it should refer only to the stumps and bails, but you will often hear it used to describe the whole pitch as well.

Figure 2 The wicket

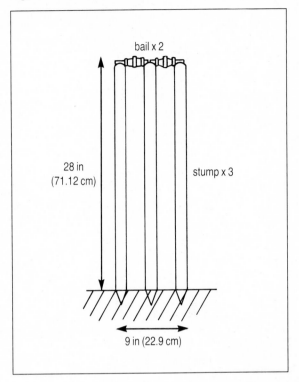

bail x 2

28 in
(71.12 cm)

stump x 3

9 in (22.9 cm)

Leg-side and off-side
You will come across these expressions frequently in cricket, so let's get to grips with them early on; they refer to positions *relative to the striker*. If you imagine a line drawn down the middle of the pitch, from the middle stump of one wicket to the middle stump of the other, everything on the same side of the line as the striker's legs is on the *leg-side*, and everything on the same side as the bat is on the *off-side*. Remember that it is the striker's position that determines which is which. What is leg-side when a right-handed striker is at the wicket automatically becomes off-side when the right-hander is replaced by a left-hander at the same wicket.

Each time six fair balls have been delivered from one end, a different bowler takes over at the other. This is called *the change at the end of an over*, and the fielders are repositioned to provide the best possible defence against the fresh striker.

All clear? Keep that in mind for when we look more closely at the progress of a game on page 40.

2

Equipment

The bat

The bat must be made of wood. The maximum length allowed is 38 inches (96.5 cm), and it must not be wider than 4.25 inches (10.8 cm). The blade of the bat is normally made from willow, and the handle from cane. The handle will usually have one or more strips of rubber inserted down its length; these are known as the *springs*, and provide a cushioning effect. A grip (made of cord and rubber) completes the bat. Beginners should not buy a bat before getting some experience in the game – it will take some time to discover what size and weight will suit you best.

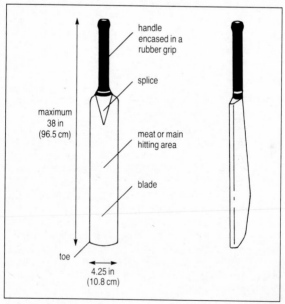

handle
encased in a
rubber grip

splice

maximum
38 in
(96.5 cm)

meat or main
hitting area

blade

toe

4.25 in
(10.8 cm)

Figure 3 The bat

It is very common for juniors to try to play with a bat which is too large — either because they want to feel "grown up", or because misguided parents give them one which will "allow for growth". Whatever the motive, it won't help the child, because it makes the development of a natural batting style almost impossible. As a general rule, if the top of the handle of the bat is no more than an inch (2.5 cm) higher than your inside-leg measurement, the size will be about right.

Bats come in quite a wide range of weights as well as sizes. Beginners will usually play better with a relatively light bat.

The ball

Cricket is played with a hard ball made from thick leather stitched over a core of cork bound very tightly with cord. The main feature of the ball is the *seam*, where the two halves of the leather cover are sewn together. The seam is rough, and can be used by the bowler to have a marked effect on both the flight and the bounce of the ball.

Leather balls are quite expensive, and it is common for plastic or "composition" balls to be used for practice and informal play.

A cricket ball should weigh between 5.5 and 5.75 oz (156–163 g), and have a circumference of between 8.812 and 9 inches. Smaller and lighter balls are used for juniors, starting at about 4 oz (113 g).

In most forms of indoor cricket, a softer ball is used which is similar to a tennis ball enclosed in a leather jacket.

Clothing

The traditional clothing for outdoor cricket is white and consists of a shirt, long trousers and boots with spiked soles. The spikes are a great help in making rapid changes of direction on grass. A peaked cap and a sweater usually complete the outfit. However, clothing conventions are changing, and in warm climates lightweight cotton clothing is now common. Shorts are often worn by both men and women, and floppy sun-hats are increasingly popular.

Do use boots rather than shoes. This is important, because knocks on the ankles are surprisingly common in cricket, and a ball hitting the unprotected bone just above the ankle is quite extraordinarily painful! Wear two pairs of socks with your boots to keep your feet from becoming blistered or sore.

In the forms of indoor cricket in which a softer ball is used, things are usually very free and easy, and any form of sports clothing is acceptable. The only essential requirement is that you do not wear shoes with black rubber soles which will mark the floor of the playing area.

Clothing for any type of cricket should fit easily and not restrict movement at all.

Protection

A hard cricket ball, which may travel at up to 100 mph (160 kph), can cause injury, so a basic level of protection is essential. Batters and wicket-keepers wear pads which cover their legs.

Batting gloves protect the batter's hands and fingers, and wicket-keepers wear special gloves with padded palms and extra protection for the wrists.

Boys and men *must* wear an abdominal protector (*box*) to avoid the agony of a blow to the genitals.

Extra padding for thighs and hips is available, but you will not need to invest in this until you are playing the game seriously at club level.

Helmets are a matter of personal choice; some batters find that they can only face fast bowling with confidence if they are wearing one. Whatever choice of helmet you may eventually make, you must be sure that it fits properly and does not restrict your vision in any way. Above all, it must all be made from a shatter-proof material; polycarbonate is generally used.

3

The basic skills

Catching

Catching a moving object is easy if you stick to this rule: *keep your eyes focused on it until it is safe in your hands.*

1

Although a cricket ball is hard, when you are catching it, treat it as though it were a fresh egg. Don't snatch at it — cushion it within your grasp and move your hands with it towards your body. Use both hands whenever possible, and make sure that your fingers never point directly at the flight of the ball. This way you will not hurt yourself and will hold the catch.

Catching a high ball
Hands together at eye level; fingers pointing as low as possible (photo 1).

Catching a straight close ball
Hands together in front of body; fingers pointing downwards (photo 2).

2

Catching a ball to one side
Hands together, fingers pointing to the side (photo 3).

Note how the fingers *never* point at the ball. This is an essential safety rule.

3

Throwing

Throwing fast and accurately is a vital skill for cricketers. You probably think that you can throw quite well already, but with some practice you will almost certainly be able to improve. Here is the most effective technique: it makes sure that your whole body puts energy into the throw — not simply your arm.

The trick is to have your body sideways-on to the target at the start of the throw (photo 4).

Point towards your target with your forward (free) arm as you take your throwing arm back, and rock your weight onto the rear foot (photo 5).

When you have rocked back as far as you can, push your throwing arm forwards fast, at the same time squaring up to the target and moving forward onto the other foot (photo 6).

Release the ball as your throwing arm reaches its full extension, and clear your free arm out of the way. All your weight is transferred to your forward foot, and you should continue with a follow-through. A short pace as the back foot oversteps the forward one completes the throw.

4

5

6

Practise by trying to throw a ball level, parallel to the ground, from a fixed point, and see how the distance improves as you perfect your timing. Keep practising until you can sight your target and hit it every time in a single fluid series of movements.

Throwing level is a really good indicator of how much power you are getting into the throw. Practise throwing for maximum distance too, by aiming towards the sky with the free arm and releasing the ball at a higher angle (45° for best effect), but remember that once you start playing cricket properly, accuracy and control will often be more useful to you than all-out distance.

Fielding

No matter how good you may be as a batter, if you are to be an asset to your team, you must be able to play your part as a good fielder too. If the ball is in the air near to you, you must do all you can to get the striker out by catching it. If the ball is on the ground, you have to stop the batters making runs by getting it back to the wicket as fast as you can. Throwing and catching are two of the main skills of a fielder, but you must also learn to be good at stopping a ball running along the ground, and develop the art of knowing which end of the pitch to return it to.

You must learn the safe way to stop a ball which is coming along the ground towards you. The position is called the *long barrier* (see photo 7). Your weight should be on the foot on the same side as the arm you prefer to throw with. Bend your other leg, so that the knee is by the heel on the ground. Your hands must be held as they are when taking a catch — *with the fingers pointing downwards, and not towards the ball.* If you get into a position where you are looking along the line of the ball rolling towards you, you can be confident that you will stop it. Even if you miss it with your hands, you will stop it with your foot, leg or body.

The long barrier position also has the advantage of allowing you to pick up the ball and throw it with the minimum delay.

It is easy to get nervous when a ball is coming towards you and you know that everyone is looking for *you alone* to stop it. It is all too easy to become over-eager and to snatch at the ball. Don't do it! Keep calm, and hold the position described above. Attempts to reach forward to the ball will often result in painfully bruised fingers, or the ball being deflected up into your face. If you stay in the proper position these dangers will be safely avoided.

Of course, there will be many occasions when you will be chasing a ball, or may just be able to get to it from the side. At these times you need common sense, agility and the ability to dive full-length onto the grass!

Good reactions are important in the field; players with fast reactions are usually placed quite close to the pitch, where the chances of a catch are increased. The closest positions are the *slips*, which are behind the striker's off-side (see page 9). This is a good position to catch balls which just glance off the side of the bat, but fast reaction speed is needed. The various positions on the field, and the strange names given to them, are explained on page 47.

You can still be a valuable fielder if your reactions are not super-fast. A reliable player further away, who can throw powerfully and accurately, can have plenty of opportunities to save runs and help take wickets.

Bowling

If you become a good bowler, you will always be in demand on the cricket scene. But whether you develop immense speed, or concentrate on the crafty techniques of spin, you need to learn the basic action first.

Bowling differs from throwing in one essential: the bowling arm must be *swung* to deliver the ball. *You*

*are not allowed to straighten your arm during the final
part of the delivery swing.* If you do, you are consider-
ed to be throwing the ball, and will be liable for penalty under the "no ball" rules (see page 43).

Basic bowling action

Let's take a look at basic bowling practice: for this
session your target is to be the top of a stump which
is about twenty metres away from you. You are aiming to make the ball bounce once before hitting the
top of the stump. Obviously, this practice is a lot more
fun if there are at least two of you bowling at stumps
set at opposite ends of a pitch.

Bowling starts with a good grip. Here's a typical
grip to use: the ball is held resting on the pad of the
thumb, with the first two fingers extended each side of
the seam. The other two fingers are tucked towards
your palm (photo 8).

8

The principle of being sideways-on to the target
applies in just the same way as it does for throwing.
If you are bowling correctly, you will have your free
side facing the target as you start, and will end up
with the shoulder of your bowling arm facing it at the
finish.

19

Start off like this, with your free arm pointing vertically above your head, and the hand holding the ball just under your chin.

Figure 4

Remember: *keep looking at the target throughout the bowling sequence.*

Now raise your forward leg, pointing at the sky with the toe, and lean your body back as far as you dare. This is sometimes called the *coil* position. You are now ready to start the delivery.

Figure 5

Pull the ball from under your chin and "unwind" your arm so that the hand holding the ball follows the path of a figure "6", at the same time starting to stamp down with your forward foot.

Figure 6

While your bowling arm has been rising up behind you, your free arm is moved forwards and down in a smooth arc passing alongside your body.

You should release the ball when your hand is as high as it will go, right at the top of the "6".

Figure 7

Don't stop now! You must continue with a smooth "follow-through"; your bowling arm should continue in its circular path until it has crossed in front of your body and ended up almost under the opposite armpit. If you are putting any effort into your bowling, you will find that the free arm will end up pointing behind you, in almost exactly the opposite direction to the target.

Figure 8

Adding a run-up

So far you have been taking just one step when you bowl; once you have got your arms and legs working together in the right order, you can start to add a few paces of run-up. Don't be in too much of a hurry to do this — practise the single-step delivery until you have perfected it first. It is often helpful if you are able to practise the movements in front of a mirror, or under the eye of a more experienced friend.

Once you have developed the basic bowling action and can hit the stump target reasonably often, you can begin to add the run-up. This will automatically give a bit more speed, but you shouldn't be trying to go as fast as possible yet — even if you want to be a demon fast bowler one day! Practise getting your timing right, and build up speed gradually.

Start to add a run by finding out how many paces you feel comfortable with, and which foot you are going to start from. The easy way to do this is by turning your back to the pitch, and pretending to bowl in the opposite direction to the wickets. Starting from the bowling crease, run the number of steps which seems about right for you. Make a mark on the ground and start off from there when you make a real delivery down the pitch. You will need a few tries before you find the exact number of paces which gets you to the bowling crease on the right foot to make a perfect delivery.

After a number of attempts, you will find that one particular combination of speed and steps feels most comfortable to you. If your friends take many more steps or many less, don't worry; it is important to work at your own natural speed and rhythm.

Bowling on the pitch

You have to release the ball while your front foot is either on or behind the popping crease. As your run speeds up, your strides will lengthen, so you must allow for this as your experience increases. If you run over the popping crease, or touch the return crease at all while the ball is still in your hand, the delivery will be called a *no ball* (see page 43).

Let's look at the whole process of delivering a medium-paced ball, from start to finish: remember to keep your eye on the striker throughout the process. The sequence is illustrated on pages 24–25.

Start your run from a point which you will have marked on the ground a suitable distance behind the bowling-end wicket. You will be square-on to the striker as you run — slowly at first, then gathering speed steadily. As you approach the wicket, you make the start of the actual delivery by jumping into the air while still travelling forwards. This jump is vital: you must take off from the foot opposite your bowling arm (the left foot if you are right-handed), and turn so that your free side faces the striker and you are virtually sideways-on. The foot on the same side as your bowling arm should hit the ground just behind the bowling crease, and *almost parallel to it*. If you have got this right, you will find it easy and natural to swing your arms as you learned for the basic bowling action, and to release the ball accurately down the pitch. The follow-through will take place quite naturally, and, in fact, you will have no choice but to take an extra pace or two down the pitch. You are allowed to do this provided that you have released the ball before stepping past the popping crease. Figure 9 shows a typical pattern of the run-up and delivery for a right-handed bowler.

The type of bowling delivery you have learned will make the ball bounce straight, and you should aim it at the striker's off-stump (remember — that's the one on the off-side, as explained on page 9). Bowling becomes an art when you start to spin the ball to make it swing as it flies through the air, or bounce off the ground at an angle.

Debra Maybury delivers a medium-paced ball

9

10

11

12

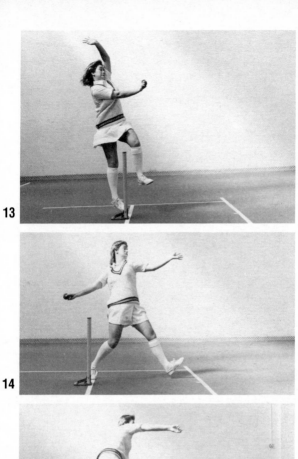

13

14

15

16

You will come across strange names for some of the different types of bowling delivery. Some of these are a matter of skill and a source of pride to the bowler. Others, such as the *beamer*, should only happen by accident, as they are dangerous. In the following descriptions, it is assumed that a right-handed batter is facing the bowling.

Beamer A fast full-pitch to the head of the striker. Not a legal ball; never try one deliberately.

Bouncer A very fast ball which pitches short and bounces to the striker's chest or head. Too many bouncers are frowned upon in club cricket.

Chinaman A ball from a left-arm spin bowler which bounces towards the leg-side.

Googly A very deceptive delivery: bowled by a right-arm bowler, it is delivered as if it is going to break to the off-side, but is spun so that it breaks to the leg.

Leg-break A ball which is spun so that it bounces from the leg-side towards the off-side.

Long-hop This would be a *bouncer* if it had been delivered very fast; as it is, it is simply a ball which is pitched short and bounces high, so that the striker has plenty of time to sight on it.

Off-break A ball which is spun so that it bounces from the off-side towards the leg-side.

Swinger A ball that swings in the air, rather than when it bounces. An *in-swinger* goes from off-side to leg-side, and an *out-swinger* from leg-side to off-side.

Top-spinner A ball delivered so that it is spinning forward through the air. It comes off the ground faster than expected after the bounce.

Yorker Any ball pitched exactly at the striker's feet. Very hard to play.

Spin

You can't really learn to be a spin bowler by reading a book, but you can get a good idea of the general techniques. After that, your progress is a matter of practice and more practice. We will start with bowling an off-break, because the ball does not have to travel fast for this to be effective — in fact the slower it is going, the more it will deviate, as it will be in contact with the ground longer when it bounces. Here's the method for a right-hander:

17

Grip the ball tightly in your palm, with your first two fingers spread as widely as is comfortable (photo 17). *Keep your wrist loose and flexible.* As you release the ball, twist your hand clockwise, in a "doorknob-opening" action. If you've got it right, the inside of your forefinger will spin the ball quite powerfully, and it will bounce from off-side to leg-side.

Figure 9 Typical pattern of run-up and delivery for a right-handed bowler

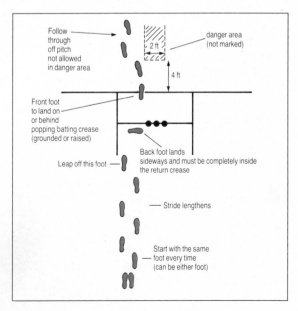

For a leg-break, the grip is similar, but your fingers should not be spread quite so widely, nor the grip be quite as tight (photo 18). As your hand reaches the top of its arc, you rotate your wrist rapidly anti-clockwise, spinning the ball with your third finger as you release it. From the striker's point of view, it will appear that it is released from over the back of your hand. You will have to try the action a few times with a soft ball to get the feel of it.

18

Swing

Swing occurs when the ball is in flight towards the striker. It is only effective for medium and fast balls. The position of the seam as the ball is bowled determines which way it will swing. If it is pointed a little to the off-side of the striker (approximately towards the *second slip* position — see page 41), the ball will swing in that direction; this is called an *out-swinger*. You do not have to be very bright to work out that if the seam is pointed at a position on the leg-side (*fine leg* — page 41 again), the result will be an *in-swinger*.

The swing can be increased if one side of the ball is rough and the other shiny. The ball is bowled with the seam aimed as described above, but with the *rough* surface on the side to which the ball is intended to swing. This is why you often see cricketers polishing the ball on their trousers.

Photo 19 shows how to grip the ball for swing. Your grip should not be too tight, but you must keep your wrist much stiffer than when spin-bowling.

19

Variation

As well as spin and swing, you can make life harder for the striker by varying the speed of delivery. Other variations are bowling to different lengths, and altering the position from which you deliver the ball. Don't overdo this last variation — it is almost always best to bowl from as close to the bowling-end stumps as possible. Of course, you cannot use variation effectively until you can bowl accurately and with good control.

Batting

Many people feel that batting is the most enjoyable part of playing cricket. Maybe they are right, because when you are batting all the game revolves around you; not only do you have to control your own skills and emotions, but you must also try to outwit the eleven players on the field who are all dedicated to getting you out at the earliest possible opportunity!

The grip

If you get into the habit of gripping the bat correctly from the start, you will also automatically have good control and be able to play safer shots. Here's how to get the right grip:

● Put the bat face-down on a chair.

- Grip the bat with your hands close together, as near the top of the handle as is comfortable, imagining that its face is the sharp edge of a two-handed axe.

- Raise the bat as if you intend to chop the chair in two. Swing it two or three times — no, you don't actually have to hit the chair!

- Without altering your grip, take up the normal batting position (photo 20).

- Confirm that your grip is correct by sighting down the line running through the Vs formed between your thumbs and forefingers. This imaginary line should run down to the ground between the splice and the outside edge of the bat (photo 21).

Below and *right*: These two photographs show how your grip should look; you will need some practice before this feels completely natural.

20

The controlling hand

When you are batting, it is the *top* hand which controls the shots. This is usually the opposite one to that which you use for the majority of your skills such as writing, catching or throwing, so don't be surprised if the batting action feels a little strange at first. You will have to concentrate − if you let the lower hand take over, you will find that you tend to hit the ball into the air most of the time, and being caught is one of the easiest ways to be out.

Facing the bowling

Take up your position at the wicket with one foot each side of the popping crease. You should be sideways-on to the bowler with your feet about 9 inches (23 cm) apart. The toe of the bat should rest lightly on the ground behind your back foot. If your stance is correct, your front shoulder will be the only one the bowler can see, but your head should face him or her with your eyes level.

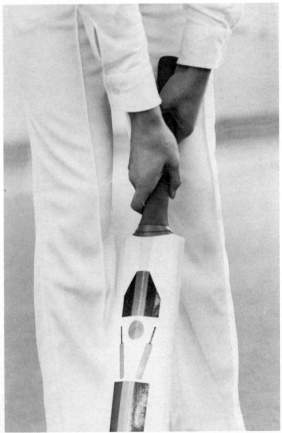

22

Paul Grayson at the wicket, ready for the first ball

The old rule about keeping your eyes on the ball is never more true than when batting. You must watch the ball as far as possible onto the bat.

It is important to be slightly relaxed; don't stand with your legs stiff and taut — let your knees bend slightly. If you find it impossible to keep your eyes level as you face the bowler, try lifting the bat off the ground a little.

Your first objective is to stay in. Don't be too ambitious for runs early on; don't expect to slog the ball to the boundary the first time you face a bowler. The key to staying in is to *play straight*. That means keeping your bat as upright as possible and playing the ball forward. Remember, when the bat is in front of the wicket, the bowler really has a very small target to hit.

23

The bowler has a very small target if you take up the correct position at the wicket

As the bowler reaches the stumps at the other end, you should lift your bat up in line with your middle stump and move your arms away from your body a little so that you are ready and in position to play the shot.

As we have said, the most common way of getting out is not by being bowled, but by giving a catch. Remember that the top hand is the controlling hand: if you keep your top hand in front of the bottom hand at the moment of impact, the ball will go down towards the ground and not up into the air. As you strike the ball, your hands should look like those of the batter in photograph 24.

Beginners' shots

How do you decide which shot to play? There are many possibilities, but at this stage in your game we will concentrate on safe ones which will increase your chances of staying at the wicket. The key is the ability to judge length — to anticipate where, and how high, the ball will bounce. This is a skill which takes time to acquire, and the time you spend practising with your friends will always pay off. You need to develop the ability to decide whether to play *forward* or to play *back* as soon as the bowler has let go of the ball.

Forward shots

A forward shot is one played with your weight on your front foot.

If you think that after bouncing the ball would hit the stumps near either the top or the bottom, then you should play *forward*: you should move your body and front leg towards the ball, bringing the bat down in a straight line, and with the top hand firmly in charge.

Now you have to make a second decision: can I reach to hit the ball with the bottom half of the bat, or can I only get the top half to it? If you reckon you can hit with the bottom half, you're really in luck! Drive forwards with both hands, towards the bowler, remembering to keep the top hand in charge, and follow through with the bat after the ball has been hit. This is called the straight drive; if played correctly, the ball will go straight past the bowler on the ground for a boundary (4 runs).

25

Straight drive

If you think that you will only be able to hit the ball with the top half of the bat, you will have to make a defensive shot. Move forwards as before, but bring the bat down in a short stroke which stops the ball just in front of your front leg. For this shot your top hand must be completely in charge and your bottom hand almost totally relaxed.

Forward defensive shot, with the top hand well forward

26

A back-foot shot

If you judge that the ball is going to bounce over the top of the wicket, you should take a small pace backwards, nearer to the stumps, and transfer your weight onto your back foot. Make sure that your top hand is in control as usual, and in front of the relaxed lower one.

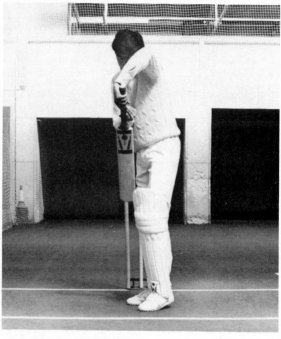

27

Back foot defensive shot

If you can play these shots, then you can survive — remember you can only score runs for as long as you can keep your team batting, so to stay in is your first priority!

More ambitious strokes

Once you can protect your wicket, and have begun to judge length fairly reliably, you can be rather more ambitious with your choice of stroke. The rule is still to keep the ball on the ground and the bat straight.

Drives

Figure 10 shows a range of drives, which are all developed from the basic forward stroke which you learned earlier. As usual, you control the angle of the blade with your top hand.

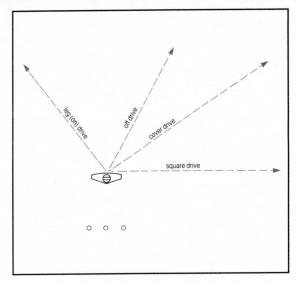

Figure 10 Forward drives (angles of bat not shown)

Strokes off the back foot

You can score useful runs even when the length of the ball forces you to play off the back foot. You can't get so much power into these shots, but you can try any of the drives mentioned above, as well as some crafty deflection shots such as the leg-glance and the off-glance.

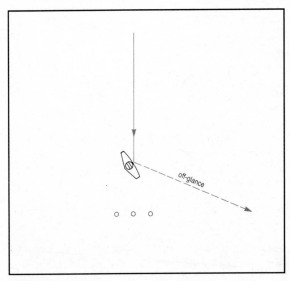

Figure 11 The off-glance

The pull

The pull is a useful shot to use if the bowler presents you with a long hop, but don't fall into the trap of trying it until you have received a few balls and have got the feel of both the pitch and the bowling.

To play the pull, you will have to abandon your side-on stance, and face the bowler squarely. Take a small step backwards with your back foot (the foot nearest the stumps), at the same time turning it so that the toe faces the bowler. Now move the other foot in the same direction, bringing your chest square to the bowler. The stroke is made with your weight on your back foot, and the ball is hit towards the square-leg umpire (see page 41). Take care to angle the shot downwards — it is quite easy to send it high for an easy catch.

The square cut

The square cut is another cross stroke. It is used to best effect (and most safely) on a ball which is wide of the off-stump and short of a good length. To play the square cut, you move your back foot across towards the ball, the other foot following through as you make the stroke. Your back will turn towards the bowler slightly, and the ball is hit towards the cover-point position (page 41).

The advice to keep your eye on the ball, right up until you hit it, is extra important when making cross strokes.

28

38

Wicket-keeping

A good wicket-keeper needs agility, anticipation and courage! Of all the fielders, the wicket-keeper has the most opportunities for stopping runs and getting batters out. Normally, the 'keeper will face every ball, changing ends after each over.

The 'keeper must stay behind the stumps until the striker has touched the ball. For slow and medium bowling, the best position is very close to the stumps, and just to the off-side. Fast bowling means that the 'keeper must stand farther back, where the ball can be taken comfortably between knee and waist height.

From this position you should be able to "put down" the wicket if the striker gets out of the crease through playing forward but missing the ball. You will also be well placed to take catches off the edge of the bat.

Although the correct expression for disturbing the wicket is to say that it has been "put down", all that is needed is to remove a bail. Remember, you don't *have* to knock the bail off with the ball itself — you can use the hand, or the arm of the hand, holding the ball.

If for any reason the bails are already off the wicket, then it may be put down by the wicket-keeper (or a fielder) pulling a stump out of the ground with the hand holding the ball.

Left and **below**: *The keeper in position for a slow bowler. From here he can easily stump the batter if a stroke misses the ball.*

29

4

Playing the game

The teams in action

Let's assume that we have two teams of eleven players, two umpires whose job it is to see fair play, one or two scorers, a cricket field already marked out, a ball and all the bats and equipment needed to play a game.

Before we start, we need to check that each team has decided which player should be its captain. The captains are important in cricket: they decide the order in which the batters play, who shall bowl, and where they want their fielders placed.

Now that the scene is set for a battle of skill and wits, let's see how the play should take place: don't worry if some of the expressions are unfamiliar to you — we will deal with each one separately in the next section.

- The captains toss a coin to decide which team shall bowl and which shall bat.

- The *opening batters* go out to the pitch as the *bowling side* takes up position in the field.

- The captain of the bowling side will arrange the team on the field. A commonly used arrangement is shown in Figure 12.

- When the umpires are satisfied that all is ready, play starts with the bowler sending down the *first delivery* to the striker.

- If a good hit is made, the batters may decide to try and score one or more *runs*.

- One or other of the batters will *call* as the signal to run.

- If an uneven number of runs has been made, the batters will automatically have *changed ends*.

30

Tossing a coin to settle which team bats first.

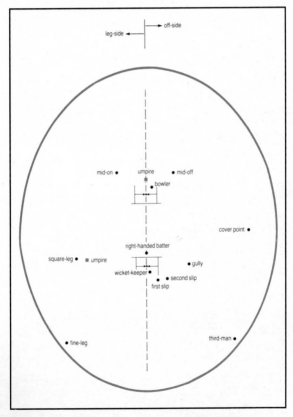

Figure 12 Typical fielding plan for a right-handed batter; this is just a sample of the many possible fielding positions

- After six fair balls have been bowled, an *over* is called, and the bowling changes ends. A different player will bowl from the other end of the pitch for another six balls. The captain of the bowling side will reposition his fielders at the end of each over. This has to be done skilfully so that they are in the best possible position both to take catches and to stop runs.

- Maybe the bowler will be successful in hitting the wicket and the striker will be *bowled out*. There are many other ways of being *out*, when the fielders have to *appeal*, and these will be explained in the next section. The batter who is out is replaced by the next member of the batting team.

- Once a side has ten of its players out, or when the agreed number of overs have been bowled (see page 45), the teams change places, and the whole process is repeated.

- Apart from the runs scored by the batters actually running between the wickets, there will be those given for *boundaries*, and *extras*, which can be gained in a number of ways. The team with the greatest number of runs is the winner. The batter with the greatest number of runs will be a hero or heroine for at least a couple of hours, and a wonderful afternoon will have been had by everyone.

The terms explained

First delivery

Not too hard to work out! This is the first ball of the match, and will be faced by the *opening bat*.

31

The batter is ready to run as a left-handed bowler delivers a slow ball.

42

Runs

Cricketing success is measured in runs. The simplest form of run is a "single", which is scored when the batters manage to run down the pitch between the popping creases before the fielders can break either of the wickets with the ball. There is no need for the ball to have been hit — the batters can run even if neither of them has touched it (see *byes*, page 44). They can continue to run back and forth between the creases as many times as they dare, as long as the ball is still "in play". The toe of the bat must be grounded behind the crease at the end of each run. Normally, the ball becomes *in play* as soon as the bowler starts to run, and becomes *dead* again when it is safely in the hands of the wicket-keeper or bowler, or when it reaches the boundary. The ball also becomes dead as soon as a batter is *out*. An umpire can also declare the ball dead in a number of special circumstances such as injury to a player, the ball being accidentally dropped by the bowler, or when the bails fall off the stumps without being touched.

As well as runs which are made by the physical act of running, they can be scored by hitting the ball to the boundary, and by being awarded "extras".

Boundaries

The expression *boundary* refers to the actual boundary around the field, and to the score for a ball that passes over it.

Six runs are given if the ball passes over the boundary without bouncing (it's allowed to touch a fielder on the way), and four runs if it gets there having bounced or rolled.

Don't fail to run unless you are absolutely certain that the ball will reach the boundary.

If a boundary occurs as a result of an *overthrow*, you score the number of runs you have already made, as well as the allowance for the boundary. For example, suppose you had already run three times before a fielder threw the ball so that it ran over the boundary, your score would be 3 + 4 = 7 runs. In such cases it is not even necessary for the batters to complete their final run — provided they have crossed at the moment the fielder throws the ball, they will be credited with it.

Extras

The usual extras are runs given because the bowler delivers a *no ball* or a *wide*. In either case a run is awarded to the batting side if they fail to score any other way from the delivery. A *no ball* is called by the umpire at the moment of delivery, and is usually due to a foot-fault by the bowler, or to the ball having been thrown instead of properly bowled. A batter cannot be bowled or caught out from a no ball, but there is the danger of being *run out* if an attempt is made to score from it in the normal manner.

Wides are balls which an umpire considers are out of reach of a striker who is standing normally at the wicket — either too high or too far to one side. If the striker makes an effort to hit a wide which puts him or her within range of it, a wide will not be given.

Byes are the runs scored by running even though the striker made no contact with the ball. This is often possible, particularly if the wicket-keeper misses it too. Sometimes a ball from a fast bowler will travel to the boundary without any help from the batting side, in which case four byes are scored.

Leg byes occur when the ball is deflected by the striker's body or clothing, rather than by the bat or a hand holding it. The striker has to have made an attempt to play the ball, or to be taking genuine avoiding action. The runs have to be made in the same way as if the ball had been hit with the bat, but on the scoresheet they are entered as *leg byes*.

Calling

The decision of whether to run or not is an important one for the batting side, and it should never be left to guesswork. It is the responsibility of the batter with the best view to *call* the run. This means that if you hit the ball in front of you, then you should call, but if the ball goes past and behind you, your partner at the other end should call.

Always make the call loud, clear and decisive: **"yes"**, **"no"**, or **"wait"**.

As you pass your partner during the run, you can exchange information — there may be the chance of one or two more runs if you keep your wits about you. Don't miss the chance to take an extra run if the fielding side *overthrows*, in other words, if one of them throws the ball hard and the wicket-keeper or bowler misses it so that it runs over the other side of the pitch. Accurate calling when such opportunities come is vital.

Ends

The bowler bowls from the *bowling end* of the pitch, and the striker operates at the *batting end*. After each *over* of six balls, the ends change, and bowling is done from the other end. The only time the batters change ends is while making runs. If an uneven number of runs is scored, a different batter will face the bowling for the next ball, unless the runs were scored off the last ball of an over. In this case the previous batter will be facing a new bowler.

If the batters have made some runs off a ball which turns out to be a boundary, they return to the ends they started from, because a boundary is always an even number of runs.

Overs

Each bowler delivers six fair balls in an over (or eight balls in some matches). Wides and no balls are not counted as part of the over. A bowler cannot bowl two consecutive overs, but that is the only restriction on how often they bowl. The bowling end changes at the end of each over.

When the match is to be played for a limited number of overs (an *overs match*), it is usual to restrict the number of overs which any player can bowl.

One of the umpires' jobs is to keep count of the number of balls bowled, and to call "over". Umpires usually carry six pebbles or coins which they transfer from one pocket to another as the balls are bowled.

32

Over! Fielders and umpires change position.

Out

There are many ways a batter can be out. Here we will deal with the ones you are most likely to meet:

Bowled Simple: the bowler bowls a ball which hits the stumps so that one or both of the bails fall. It makes no difference whether the striker has touched the ball or not.

Hit wicket This is the verdict if the striker hits the wicket and dislodges the bails with bat, body or clothing while making a shot. However, if you hit a wicket accidentally while running between them for runs, you are not out.

45

Caught The striker is out if the ball is hit with the bat (or the hands holding the bat) and is caught by a member of the other side before it touches the ground. The fielder has to be inside the boundary throughout the catch. The ball is allowed to touch an umpire or another fielder before being finally caught. The only exception to this is if it happens to bounce off a fielder's protective helmet.

If a catch is taken, but in doing so the fielder touches or steps over the boundary, the batter is not out, and has scored a *boundary six.*

Out! – caught behind wicket.

33

Run out A batter is run out if, when attempting a run, the wicket is broken with the ball by the fielding side before the batter has grounded either bat or feet over the popping crease.

It is usually quite clear which batter is out, but if there is any doubt, the matter is settled by deciding whether they have crossed or not. If they have crossed, then it is the batter who is running towards the broken wicket who is out; if they have not crossed, the one who has left the broken wicket is out.

You are allowed to break the wicket with the ball, or with the hand of the arm holding the ball.

Stumped If the wicket-keeper gathers a ball and breaks the wicket when the striker is in front of the popping crease, the striker is out, stumped. The wicket-keeper can only do this from behind the wicket, unless the batter or the bat has touched the ball, in which case the 'keeper can take the ball in front of the wicket.

Leg before wicket (LBW) The LBW rule is quite complicated, but this simple explanation is a practical guide to play to:

If the ball hits the striker on any part of the body (including clothing, pads etc.) except the hands holding the bat, and if in the umpire's opinion the ball would otherwise have hit the stumps, then the player is out.

The main point of LBW is to prevent batters from using their pads to protect the wicket.

46

Appeal

The umpires decide whether a batter is out or not, but they must usually be asked. Except when the batter is bowled out, someone from the fielding side must ask *How's that?* This usually becomes shortened to a cry of *Owzat!* Make an appeal only when you genuinely think a batter is out fairly — frequent incorrect appeals become very boring.

Fielding positions

On page 41 we showed a fairly typical general-purpose field setting. There are many other positions, which you will learn gradually as you play the game. Don't be put off by the strange names of some of the positions — you don't need to learn them all at once. The main point to know is how you tell which is the *off*-side and which is the *leg*-side of the field. Remember — the side the bat is on when the striker is standing ready to face the bowling is the off-side, and the backs of his or her legs point to the leg-side. Once you have that firmly in mind, many of the positions are self-explanatory, and so if the captain asks you to go to *mid-off*, then you will be able to go to a position that is midway on the off-side. If in doubt, don't be afraid to ask, and don't imagine that the positions are accurate to a foot or two; when you get to the general area of where you think you should be, look at the captain, who will often make extra adjustments.

34

The view from third-man position, behind the slips at a village match. All eyes are on the ball. In this case the batter is a right-hander who has just attempted an ambitious leg drive. The fielder on the left of the picture is in the mid-wicket position. Try to get into the habit of working out the fielding positions every time you see a picture of a cricket match.

Umpires and umpiring

In an ideal world, there will be two umpires on the field who will have a complete knowledge of the laws of the game and will apply them with total fairness. Do not be too disappointed if this does not always happen! The usual arrangement is for each team to provide one umpire, but quite commonly this system breaks down, and players from the batting side take turns to do the job.

One umpire stands just behind the wicket at the bowling end, and the other at the batting end, in the position known as *square leg*. This is a few yards from the striker, on the leg-side. Normally the bowling-end umpire is the one who calls the "no balls" and gives judgement on LBW appeals. At the end of each over, it is usual for the umpires to remain at the same ends of the pitch, simply moving a few yards to suit their changed roles.

The laws of the game

Whoever ends up umpiring needs true familiarity with the laws of the game — something which is often sadly lacking among players! The laws have evolved over hundreds of years, and are published by the Marylebone Cricket Club (MCC). They are too extensive to include in a small book like this. As well as explaining the finer details of the rules of play, they cover every aspect of the game, including such matters as exactly when the pitch can be rolled or what to do if a bowler is incapacitated partway through an over.

5

Fitness and practice

General fitness

You will always enjoy the game more if you are fit. Although you do not need the highly-tuned fitness of an athletics competitor, you will be able to react more quickly and run faster if you have good flexibility and are not overweight. You can do basic fitness exercises at home. Coupled with a well-balanced diet, they will keep you at a good level of all-round fitness which will benefit you far beyond the cricket field. If you want to undertake a more strenuous training regime, you should plan it with the help of a qualified coach.

Frequent running at medium pace is a good all-round exercise. Run on grass if possible, and gradually build up to fairly strenuous half-hour sessions three or four times a week.

As well as basic general fitness, you will need plenty of practice in the skills of the game. Frequent training in batting, bowling and throwing will certainly lead to improvement in your ability to keep playing on the field without becoming tired (stamina). Fatigue is a sure way to make your skill level decrease; a fit, well-practised player is less likely to be careless, even when going in to bat towards the end of a long match. If you are tired, it is very easy for your first over to be the only one you get!

Exercises for batters
Repeatedly squeeze and relax on a squash ball to strengthen your grip for batting. You can do this any-where and any time, and will soon find that it can im-prove the control of your "top" hand.

Another wrist-strengthener is to hit a soft ball against a wall, holding the bat in your top hand only. You should be about ten paces from the wall, and hit the ball with a driving shot; if you hit it square, it should come straight back for you to hit again. Keep it going for as long as you can.

49

Batters need to develop a strong but flexible neck, so that they can keep their head square and eyes level as they face the bowler. Try rotating your head quite slowly in as full a circle as possible, twenty times to the right, then twenty to the left.

Weight-training warning

Note that young players should *not* do any training involving weights. Such activities should be left until the very late teens, when bone development is complete.

Warm-up

Before you go out to bat or are put on to bowl, try and do a short warm-up and stretching routine. This gives some protection against injury to muscles and tendons. Before bowling, a little jogging is also useful, because it helps you to get into the right rhythm for the first ball.

Youngsters can learn many of the skills of cricket by playing just for fun with a soft ball. **35**

Practice routines

Cricket players are fortunate because practice of the skills of the game — particularly bowling and catching — can be developed into team activities which are also good fun. If these activities are carried on at a good pace, they can help to build up fitness too. Because cricket is a team game, it is especially important to join in these sessions; you do not want to "let the side down" because you haven't paid enough attention to fitness or practice. Try these:

Catching practice

Use a soft ball. Two players stand a few yards away from a wall at least 10 ft (3 m) high. One of the players should be about two paces behind the other. The back player throws the ball at the wall, and the front one must catch it. Play as fast and as hard as you can, and change positions without stopping after every three throws. This is surprisingly strenuous, and because the front player cannot see the exact direction from which the ball will next appear, is a great game for sharpening up your reflexes.

Another good catching practice is a coaching version of French cricket. A number of players stand in an arc and throw a ball to the coach, who hits it back to be caught each time. The ball should be thrown at about knee height, and a skilled coach will ensure that it is returned at a great variety of speeds and angles.

Slip routine

For this you need a skilled coach or batter, a feeder, and five or six players. The feeder stands in front of the batter, and the players in a shallow arc behind. The feeder throws the ball hard towards the batter, at chest height. The batter just nicks the ball, causing it to be slightly deflected on its way to the players.

Net practice

Batting

Make the most of any batting practice you can get in the nets. Usually the programme means that you will get a ten-minute session, and you must use it effectively. Because you are not going to be "out" during those ten minutes, there is a tendency to slog at every

36

ball that comes towards you. It's great fun, but won't teach you anything! Treat the session exactly as you would a real innings at the wicket, and concentrate on trying to improve your game. Ask the coach if the bowlers can bowl to your particular weaknesses, and take your time; don't let the bowlers rush you.

Whenever you are batting at the nets, wear the full protective equipment — you cannot develop your true style if you are worried about getting hurt all the time. Remember, only *proper* practice makes perfect.

Bowling

As when batting, when you are bowling at the nets, you should set yourself the same standards as you would set in a match. Take care not to bowl for too long, and always remember these bowler's rules:

- I must take wickets
- I must not concede runs

Of course, there will be times when you will not be able to do this — for example, when your coach is trying to teach you a new technique. However, do set yourself high standards, and stick to them whenever possible.

Indoor cricket

The recent development of indoor cricket, as organised at numerous centres, has changed many people's attitudes to the game. Whereas the full-sized outdoor game demands lots of time and commitment if it is to be played well, it is far easier to "play at" indoor cricket and still get great satisfaction from it.

There are basically two types of indoor cricket facility, and netting is a feature of both of them; the serious indoor schools try to keep as close as possible to the skills of the outdoor game. They offer excellent opportunities for year-round net practice, and are widely used by players of all standards.

There are also the indoor cricket centres which provide everything needed to play what has become a popular and specialised form of the game. A fairly soft ball is used. Runs are scored by hitting the ball into special areas marked on the nets around the wicket, as well as by actually running. All the batting is done at one end of the pitch, the batters alternating at each over, until they have played their share (see below). The bowler changes with each over, too. Sixteen overs a side is the ration.

Usually there are eight players to a side, and everyone bowls for two overs in each innings and also shares the batting for four overs. The biggest single difference between this and the full game is that the batters have "lives". Each time you lose your wicket in the indoor game, you continue to bat until your number of overs is finished. However, there is a penalty; each time you are "out", you lose five runs. You can end up with a minus score after a vigorous but unskilled session at the wicket!

Don't dismiss this type of cricket without giving it a try. It can be tremendous fun, and provides excellent experience for players with a very wide range of ability. Split among all members of a side, the cost is quite reasonable, and everyone is sure of getting a fair share of the action.

37

The Speedball *version of indoor cricket; the scorer and umpire have a perfect view of the game.*

6

Getting into cricket

The trouble with cricket is that you simply can't play it on your own! However, the game is so popular that it is not difficult to find a club — virtually every town or village has one. As a raw beginner, you should try and join one which has an active coaching scheme. Don't be shy about approaching a club; cricketers are great enthusiasts, and are usually only too happy to welcome a newcomer to the game. Naturally, if you are a junior, you will need a club with a youth section. Do take the trouble to get a picture of the club you are joining before you commit yourself — find out just how keen they are on coaching, and whether they run regular training sessions. You will quite likely be invited to one or two of these before you join the club.

You can find a club by looking under "sports clubs" in *Yellow Pages*, and indoor schools are often listed under "sports training". If all that fails, then simply phone or write to:

The National Cricket Association
Lord's Cricket Ground
London
NW8 8QZ

Tel: 01-289 6098

and ask for the address and telephone number of either your nearest cricket club or the Secretary of your County Association.

Once you have made contact with a club, you will find that your understanding of the game will grow rapidly. Apart from a "box" for boys, you will not normally have to buy equipment straight away — most clubs keep bats, pads and gloves for general use. Clubs also frequently operate a system for passing on clothing among rapidly-growing younger members.

Be persistent, practise hard, and enjoy your cricket. Good luck!